MW00604766

Manhattan Beach

A California Beach Town

Illustrated by Gloria Judson

Written by Jane Centofante

Boardwalk Press
Manhattan Beach 2011

Manhattan Beach

A California Beach Town

First Edition

Library of Congress Control Number 2011917122
ISBN 978-0-615-53327-8
Published by Boardwalk Press
Printed and bound in the United States of America

10 9 8 7 6 5 4 3 2 1

Book design: Linda Warren, Studio Deluxe

For Grady, Hayley and Keviana,

and all of the magical memories on 34th Street

–GJ

To Dave, who seeks the endless summer,

my gratitude and love is yours always

–JC

to san francisco
HOLLYWOOD
los angeles
malibu
santa monica
MANHATTAN BEACH
N
W
E
S
catalina

Once called the "Queen of the Dunes," Manhattan Beach began as a long, quiet stretch along a southern portion of California's pristine coastline. Sandy dunes peppered with sea grasses rose up from the east only to slope gently downward to the sea. Wooden boardwalks were laid to make the journey by foot to the water's edge. Once sun seekers from Los Angeles discovered the small coastal enclave, it wasn't long before early residents planted roots to declare it a city in 1912. Over the years, it has grown to become a destination for surfing and volleyball, while trying to balance the charms of a small beach town with the desires of modern life. This book is a walk through our neighborhoods, a stroll from sandy beaches to leafy streets to a bustling downtown and beyond. All in all, Manhattan Beach remains a unique place in the hearts and minds of those who call it home by the sea.

to san diego

M
manhattan village
el porto
the tree section
the north end

The "Sections" of Manhattan Beach

El Porto... the door to endless summers and perfect waves

EL PORTO
PARKING
6:15AM-8PM

SURFBOARDS
EL PORTO
SURFBOARDS
PLAYERS LIQUOR
GR8SRF

Beach classics in the neighborhood

Pancho's
HIGHLAND

Standard bearers along Highland Avenue

The North End attracts diners, shoppers and the occasional mermaid

CAKE
BAKESHOP
WE BAKE • YOU EAT
the Local YOLK
a Beach Cafe
LOCAL YOLK
LOCAL YOLK

Sweet havens in the North End

A gathering place comes full circle...

Bruce's Beach... City Park... Bayview Terrace... Parque Culiacan... Bruce's Beach

GRANDVIEW

The challenge at Sand Dune Park

A sporting life for all seasons

MANHATTAN BEACH GRAND PRIX

The Tree Section nestled among the elms and eucalyptus

Roses bloom and wedding bells ring in Spring

The greenbelt — an old railway becomes a new trailway

through a shady grove of trees

MANHATTAN BEACH FIRE
Valley Drive
9-11-01
we shall never forget

JOSLYN COMMUNITY CENTER
city of Manhattan Beach
where civic pride intersects with parks and rec
★DORSEY FIELD★
LIVE OAK PARK

Locals' choice 24/7

THE
KETTLE
OPEN ALL NIGHT

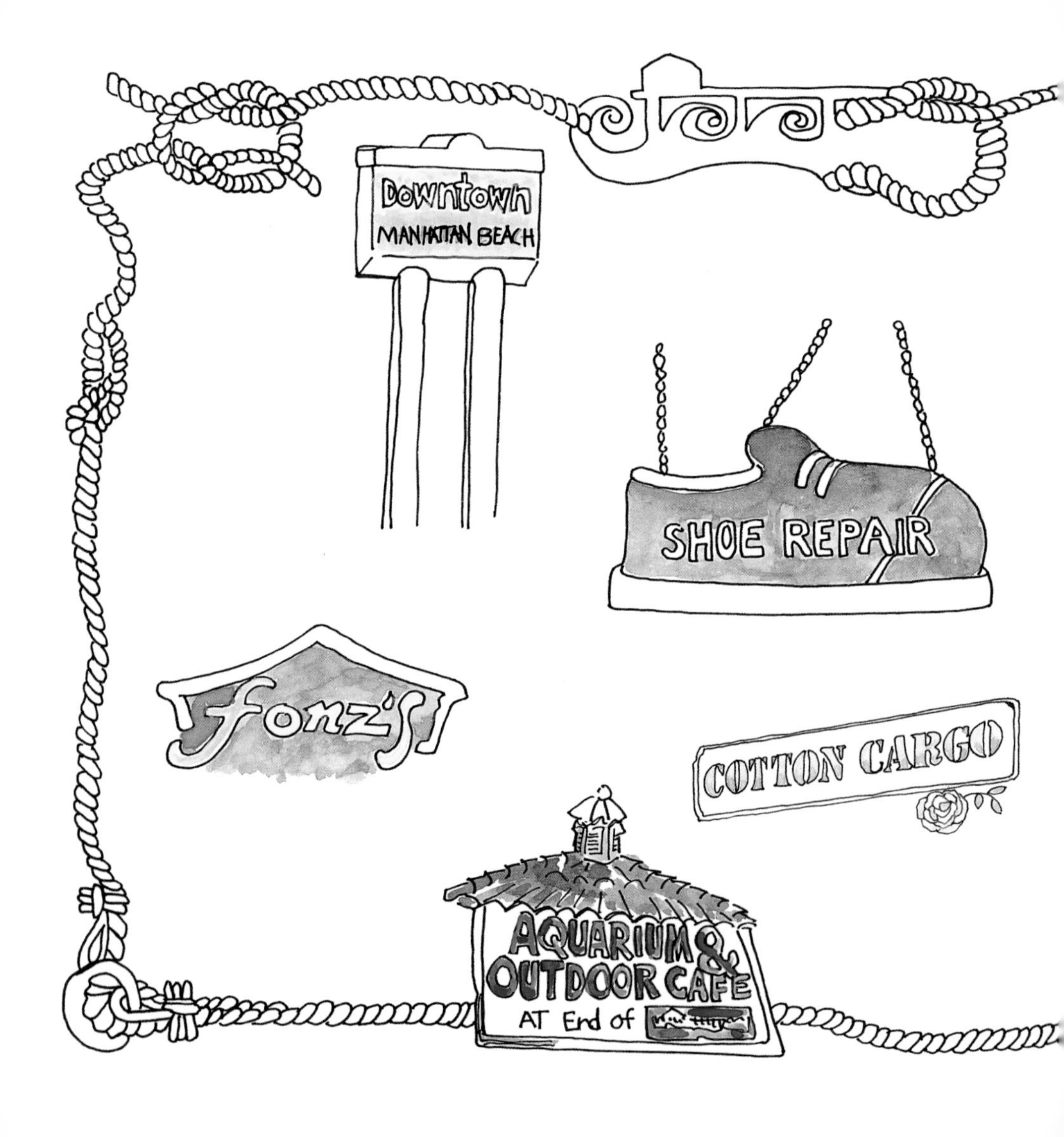
Downtown
MANHATTAN BEACH
SHOE REPAIR
fonz's
COTTON CARGO
AQUARIUM &
OUTDOOR CAFE
AT End of

THE NEPTUNIAN WOMAN'S CLUB
KOFFEE KART
Cafe
CREAMERY
MANHATTAN BEACH
TabulaRasa

A pier with peerless views

Guardians from our past...

LA MAR THEATER 1938

U.S. POST OFFICE 1933

PIER ENTRY c. 1937

MANHATTAN GROCERY c. 1910

EST. 1927
ERCOLE'S
COCKTAILS
uncle bill's
PANCAKE

Pancakes at sunrise, cocktails at sunset

Aquarium Roundhouse — an ever-present symbol

Growing Wild
1201

Awnings so bright, shopper's delight

Downtown favorites — day or night

SIDE DOOR

The Walk Streets greet the sand and surf

Collecting seashells at the shore is like gathering

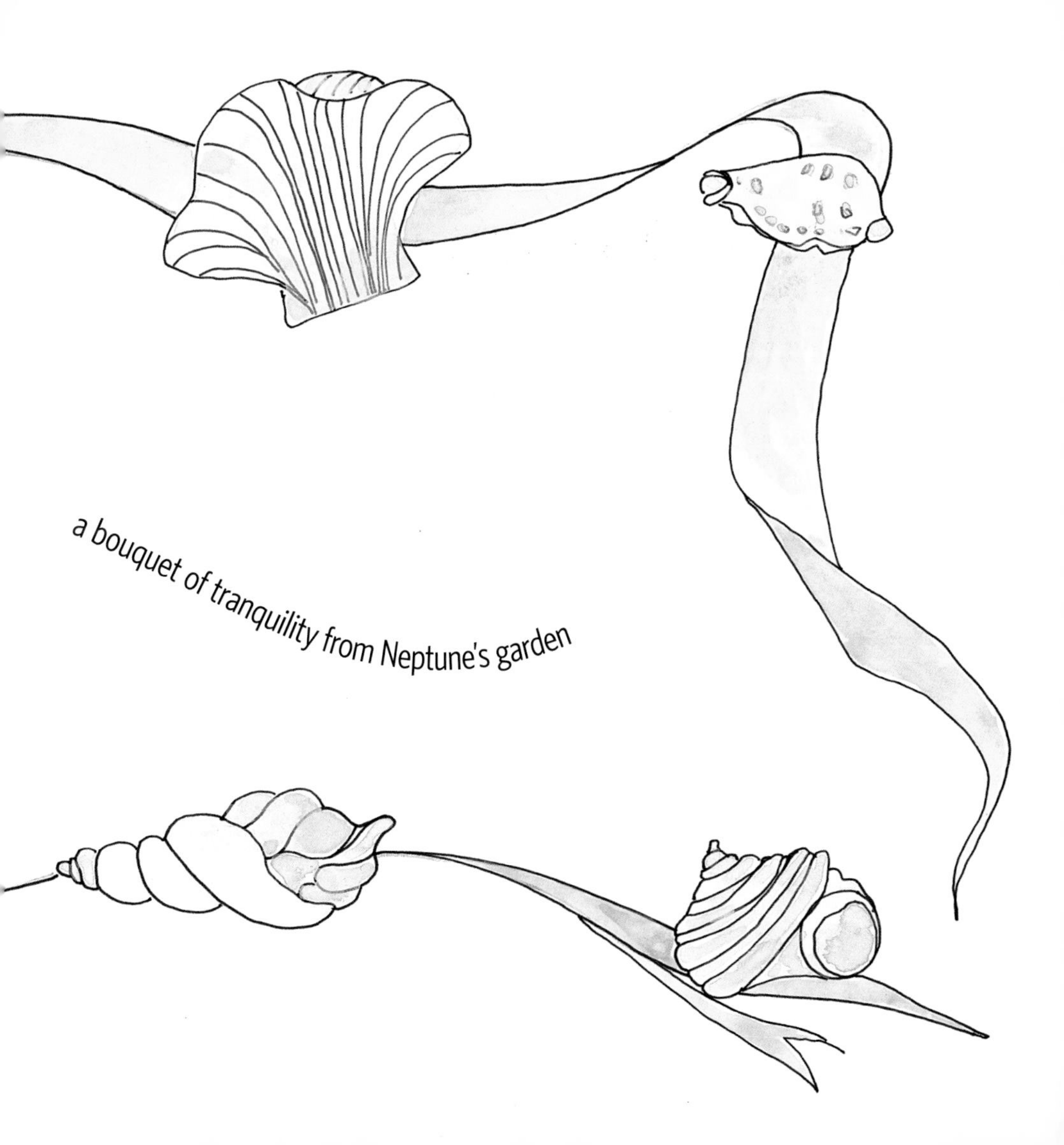
a bouquet of tranquility from Neptune's garden

California craftwork — Metlox Pottery factory 1927–1989

SHADE

Metlox Modern... treats and retreats

PETROS

Tuesdays bring the farm to the beach

The Strand — a front row seat to shimmering sea and sunsets

Manhattan Beach Open, serving since 1960

VOLLEYBALL WALK OF FAME

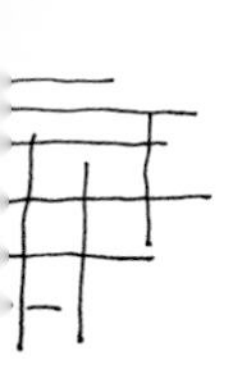

Summer porches

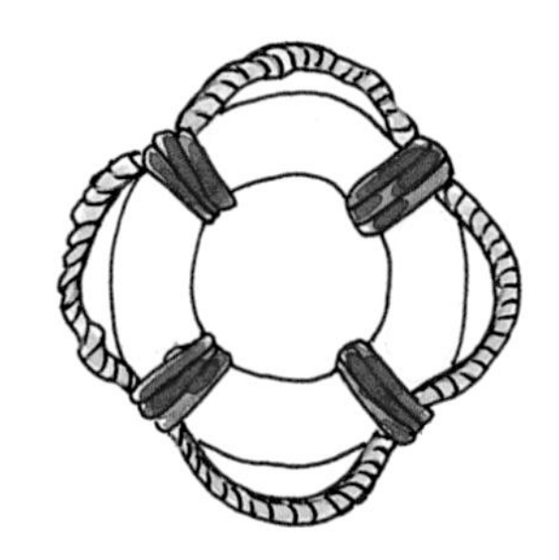

Essential beach basics make for a perfect

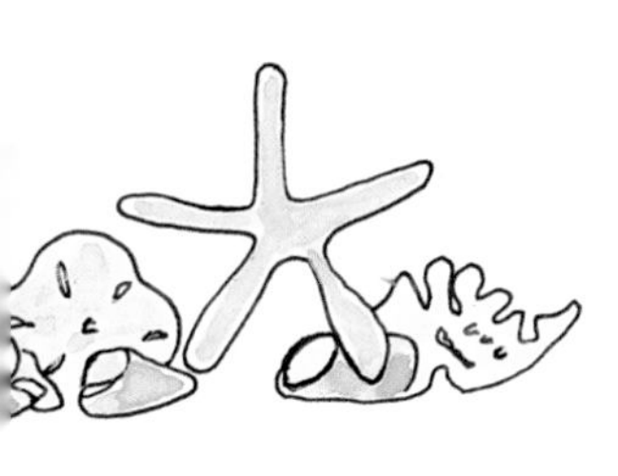

day of fun and sun at the shore

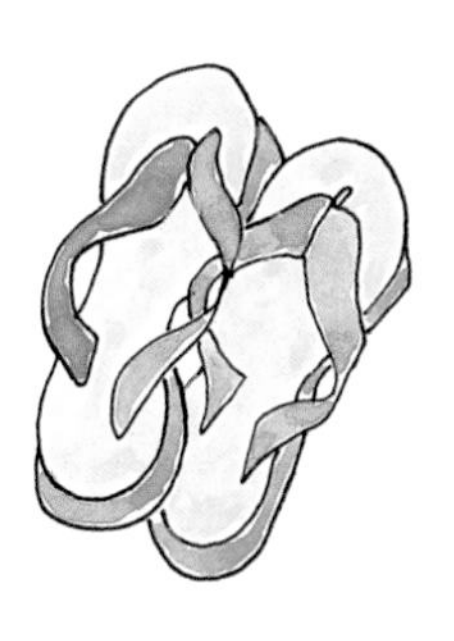

1905 COTTAGE

Picnics and concerts in the park say Summer at Polliwog

The beach goes on East of Sepulveda

SEPULVEDA

The backpack brigade!

AMERICAN MARTYRS, GRAND VIEW, MBI, MEADOWS, PACIFIC, PENNEKAMP, ROBINSON

MIRA COSTA HIGH SCHOOL

The Hometown Fair and a 10K run signal Fall is here

BEER GARDEN
welcome

Bayside vistas sparkle from the Hill Section

Holiday fireworks light the sky of a Winter's eve

Fishing for dinner... fishing for fun

Life is bliss at the beach

About the artist

Gloria Judson has been an artist and interior designer for more than thirty years, raising her children in Manhattan Beach before there was even a bike path. This is her first book of watercolor sketches. She lives on the coast in northern California with her little dog, Coco.

About the author

Jane Centofante worked as a magazine editor before taking up life as a freelance editor of non-fiction books. When not traveling to favorite old spots or wonderful new places, she lives in Manhattan Beach with her husband and their faithful bulldog, Duke.

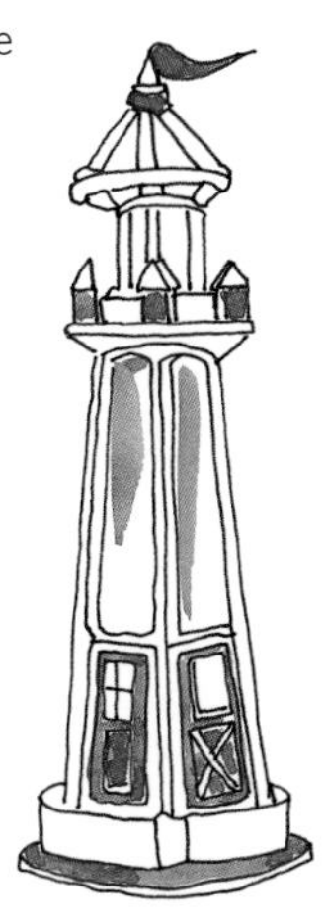

With thanks

For both of us, this book would not have happened without the love and support of so many friends and family whom we cherish. We are grateful to Kayo Ryan for generously sharing her friendships and bringing us into each other's lives, and to Anne Kasten for her ever-present wisdom and compassion.

Bringing this book to fruition was in large part due to the talents of more than a few gifted minds, and so we offer heartfelt thanks to Patricia LaVigne for her keen insights and creative solutions, to Peter Shea for always being there as a friend and an artist, and to Linda Warren and her talented colleagues at Studio Deluxe, whose collective eye for design is always beautifully expressed on the page.

Gloria thanks her parents, Virginia and Gordon Ewig, her aunt, Ann Crichton Schuman, and her cousin, Barbara Milburn, for their unfaltering love. And from Jane, with love and gratitude to her sister, Michelle Katnik, for always caring, and to her mother, Mary Centofante, who early on brought the beauty of books into her life.

And surely, this book was nurtured from conception to print by Linda Wenglikowski, sister and friend, who allowed her home to be turned into an artist studio and whose gentle care and continual sustenance of tea and cookies (and occasionally something stronger) kept us going.

We thank you all from the bottom of our hearts.